VERY, VERY, BIG!

Table of Contents

Anaconda   2

Bison   4

Tiger   6

Panda   8

Elk   10

Whale Shark   12

What A Nose!   14

Glossary / Index   16

Anaconda

What would this anaconda feel like?

This snake is an anaconda. Anacondas are the largest snakes in the world. They can grow to be up to 30 feet long. That is as long as five adults lying end-to-end.

Bison

What is this bison thinking?

Bison eat grass, so they are herbivores. This bison uses its small horns for protection. Usually, bison will run from danger. They can run faster than a horse, although they weigh more than 2000 pounds!

Tiger

What is the tiger planning to do?

The tiger is the largest member of the feline family. It hunts in Asian forests. It uses its stripes to hide in the shadows of trees and grass. This tiger also likes the snow of the cold north!

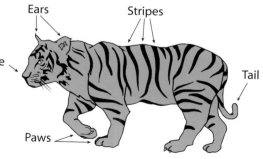

Ears   Stripes

Nose

Tail

Paws

TIGER

Panda

What would this panda say if it could talk?

See the black arms, ears, and eyes of the panda? No other bear looks like this. Panda bears are from China. They only like to eat bamboo leaves and branches. What <u>finicky</u> eaters!

Elk

Where do you think
this elk is?

Elk can weigh over a ton, as much as the bison! The young male elk's antlers can grow up to an inch a day. It would take you four months to grow that much!

Whale Shark

Describe the whale shark you see here.

Whale sharks are the largest fish in the world. Who would think they have tiny teeth? They strain their food through their gills instead of chewing. Whale sharks look polka-dotted! Their spots distinguish them from other sharks.

13

What A Nose!

Why does this picture make you smile?

This is a proboscis monkey. He is not big like the other animals in this book, but his nose is bigger than your hand! He makes a loud honking noise with his nose when he is happy.

Glossary

antlers: the horns of an elk or moose

feline: related to cats

gills: an opening in a fish's head used for breathing and eating

herbivores: animals that eat plants

Index

big nose   page   15

elk antlers   page   11

finicky eaters   page   9

largest feline   page   7

largest fish   page   13

largest snake   page   3